Pepper Grows Up
By
Darlene Luckins

About Pepper and his Family:

Pepper was one of seven ducklings raised by a mother duck in San Diego who was a very good mother. She hardly ever lost a duckling. Pepper was different from the other ducklings because he was very dark brown while his siblings were light brown and yellow. But, Pepper doesn't stay this color for his whole life as this story will show.

Pepper and his brother

Pepper has one brother with the "normal" mallard coloring of yellow and brown. But, their different appearance has no affect on them being best friends. Pepper and this brother remained best friends into adulthood and are often seen together. Pepper has a shy personality and his brother has a bold one. Pepper's brother often protected Pepper from other ducks that wanted to bully him.

Two Brothers

Ducklings and swimming

Wild ducklings often begin swimming from their first or second day. They can't produce their own oil to help them from getting too wet and sinking. When their mama sits on them to keep them warm, they get oil from her feathers. With that, they can swim and stay floating a lot longer. When they're about two weeks old, they begin to produce their own oil and also don't need mama to keep them warm as often.

Swimming Time!

Swim Time is Over

Time With Mama

What is foraging?

Foraging is just a fancy word for looking for bits of food. When ducks "forage" it means they look for food, sometimes feeling around with their bill and pick up things that look like they're good to eat. Ducklings will try to taste everything they find. Sometimes, they watch mama to see what she is eating.

Foraging

Mama duck is watchful

Some mother ducks are more protective of their babies than others. Pepper's mama was very watchful of him and he watched her, too. By watching his mother, Pepper learns what to be afraid of and what is safe. Pepper's mother also makes sounds to reassure or warn him.

Watchful
Duckling

Watchful
Mama

Best Friends

Growing Up!

Pepper begins to get real feathers

Ducklings hatch with special feathers called "down" which looks like fur. They get their real feathers starting at about ten days old. By the time they're three weeks old, they are feathered like Pepper and his brother was on the next page. Ducklings do not have all their feathers until they're at least eight weeks old.

Brothers

Nearly feathered

Pepper is nearly feathered and grown in the next photo. You can see some down on his back and his wings haven't grown out, yet. He and his brother are about six weeks old.

Getting
Big!

Pepper is now feathered

Pepper is now fully feathered in the next picture and can now fly, though he doesn't seem to like flying very much at this age. His feathers also help keep him warm and dry.

Getting adult feathers

Pepper's brown feathers began to turn gray when he was about four months old. Here is a photo of him at that time.

Almost Grown!

Pepper is now grown

Pepper and his brother are now full grown and ready for the future. Pepper will have a gray body and green head for about six months. Then, he will be dark brown again until the next spring.

All Grown Up

I hope you enjoyed watching Pepper grow up

I hope you enjoyed watching Pepper grow up. Perhaps, in your area, there is a pond or lake where you can see ducks or ducklings growing up. If you visit them, be sure to not get too close and do not chase them. If you feed the ducks, make sure you feed them healthy duck food or food like romaine lettuce or peas and NOT bread or crackers.

About the author:

Darlene Luckins lives in San Diego and spends a lot of her free time photographing ducks and ducklings as well as other birds such as shorebirds. She writes articles about nature for various websites and keeps her own blog currently known as "Killdeers, Phoebes and Finches (and Ducks!)". She is also the author of "Brave Tiny" about a brave killdeer who grows up and saves the day. "Brave Tiny" is also illustrated with colored pencil drawings by the author.